Totally Useless Skills

by Rick Davis
illustrated by Kerstin Upmeyer

...to Sisyphus

Published by Willowisp Press
801 94th Avenue North, St. Petersburg, Florida 33702

Text copyright © 1994 by Rick Davis
Covers, illustration, design copyright © 1994 by Willowisp Press,
a division of PAGES, Inc.

Printed in the United States of America

2 4 6 8 10 9 7 5 3 1

ISBN 0-87406-707-3

Contents

Introduction

Hi. Welcome to the book. I'm here to help you through it. Along the way, I'll let you in on some little secrets I know. And at the end of the book I'll tell you . . .

The BIG SECRET

So what is a Totally Useless Skill anyway?

It's something that you do that accomplishes absolutely nothing. A Totally Useless Skill won't make you money, get you a grade, or put you on the soccer team, but it WILL amaze you, impress your friends, develop your coordination, strengthen your self-confidence, and beef up your social life.

Hmm. Maybe these skills aren't so useless after all!

—Rick Davis

How to Spot a Totally Useless Skill

- Safe
- Noncompetitive
- Nonaddicting
- Requires no special equipment
- Fun!

Arm Stretching

Put both arms straight out in front of you.

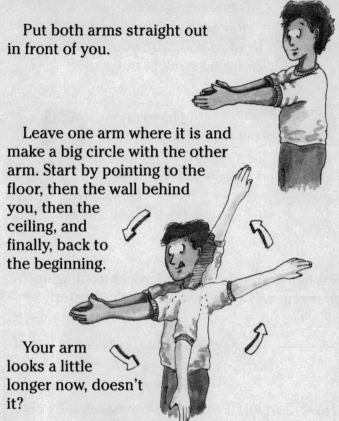

Leave one arm where it is and make a big circle with the other arm. Start by pointing to the floor, then the wall behind you, then the ceiling, and finally, back to the beginning.

Your arm looks a little longer now, doesn't it?

If you circle back the other way, your arm will return to its original size.

Arm Shrinking

Put both arms straight out in front of you, with your hands pointing straight out.

Leave one arm where it is. Now scratch your nose with your free hand.

When you put that hand out in front again, your arm will appear to be a little shorter!

Little Secret
TRY!

I know I don't have to tell you that. You obviously aren't afraid to try new things or you wouldn't be reading this book!

But some people won't try a new skill because they think they can't do it, or they don't want to risk being a failure, or they don't want to look bad.

Too bad for them, because a lot of skills are easier than they look.

Split Pencil

Using your thumbs, hold a pencil to your face at eye level. Look at it close up, like this:

Now look at something far away. Slowly rub your palms up and down together. Right in front of your very eyes, the pencil will look like it's splitting in half!

9

Disappear Your Teacher's Head

First, take a look at the X and O below.

X   O

Hold this book about 8 inches in front of you, so the X and O are at your eye level.

Close your left eye.

Look at the X with your *right* eye.

Keep looking at the X, and the O will seem to disappear!

You can do the same thing to your teacher's head.

The next time your teacher is standing near a wall, close your left eye and look at a spot on the wall, level with your teacher's head and 3 to 10 feet to the right.

If you really concentrate on that spot, your teacher's head will seem to vanish!

(If at first you don't succeed, try looking closer or farther from his head.)

Bye bye, teacher!

Little Secret
KEEP TRYING

You might not be able to do these skills the first time, so you have to keep trying.

Do you think your favorite basketball player was an instant success the first time he stepped on the court? No way. Even the best had to try again and again and again.

Mystery In The Middle

Balance a ruler on your fingers. You may put your hands at any two points.

Now slowly bring your hands together, palm to palm.

Amazingly, your fingers will always wind up under the 6-inch mark! And if you try to spread your hands apart again, only one will move!

(If you do this with a yardstick, both fingers will wind up under the 18-inch mark.)

Did You Know?

The secret to this is friction. *That's the resistance that is caused when two moving surfaces are in contact with each other.*

When the fingers on your left and right hands are equal distances from the middle of the ruler, the friction on both hands is the same, so they both move and they both arrive at the middle. But when your fingers are unevenly placed under the ruler, the friction is also uneven, and so one finger moves more easily than the other.

12

Nose Breaking

You can't graduate from school without learning this one.

Put your hands over your nose, with your thumbs near your mouth.

Now move your hands from side to side, as if you were trying to jerk your nose. At the same time, click your thumb nail on the edge of your front teeth. It will sound like your nose is breaking.

You will also hear the sound of your friends groaning.

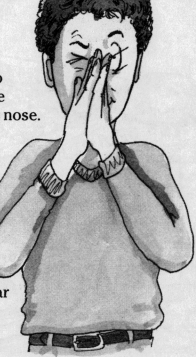

13

Balancing Act

Fold a dollar bill in half so it forms a V. (A crisp bill works best.) Stand it up on a table. Put a quarter on top, right over the V.

Grab the ends of the bill and *slowly* pull them apart so that the bill straightens out. The quarter will balance on the edge of the dollar bill.

Remember, pull very slowly.

Ghost Pencils

Cross two fingers tightly, and close your eyes.

Ask a friend to lightly rub a pencil eraser between your fingers.

It will feel like two pencils, not just one!

Normally, you *would* need two pencils to touch these two points on your fingers at the same time.

But when you cross your fingers, you need only one pencil because your brain gets fooled and thinks that two pencils are touching you.

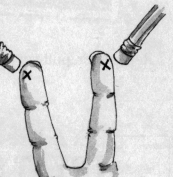

Did You Know?

There are more than 30,000 miles of nerves in your body! If placed end to end, they could go all around the world!

16

Magnetic Pencils

Press two pencil erasers together, hard.
Count to twenty.

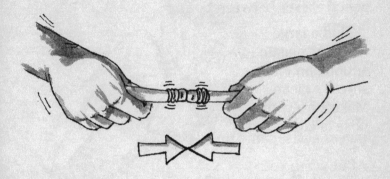

When you try to slowly move them away
from each other, the pencils will briefly feel as if
they were magnetized or stuck together.

Spoon Hanging

Never let it be said that you went through life without hanging a spoon from your face. Here's how to do it:

Find a large metal or plastic spoon and make sure it's clean. Make sure your nose is clean, too!

Breathe heavily on the spoon to make it warm and moist.

Then press the spoon hard against your nose.

Tilt your head up slightly. Hold still, and let go.

If you've come this far, why stop? Try hanging spoons from your cheeks and your chin.

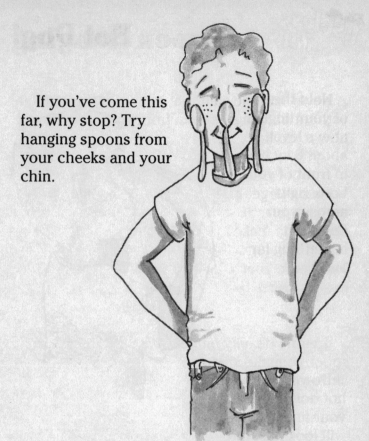

Little Secret
TRY NEW WAYS

If you're having trouble doing a skill, think of new ways to try it. In spoon hanging, for example, try tilting your head at different angles. Try warming the spoon longer. Or try a bigger spoon.

Hot Dog!

Hold the tips of your fingers at eye level, about 6 inches in front of you. Look right across your fingers at something far away.

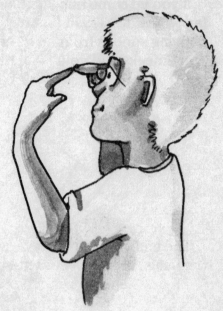

Do you see a hot dog between your fingers? It will look like this:

If you hold your fingers like this, you'll see a ball floating in space.

If you hold your fingers like this, you'll see a heart.

If you hold your fingers like this, you'll see a snowman.

The image your right eye sees is overlapping the image seen by your left eye.

Did You Know?

You are either right-handed or left-handed, right? But did you know that you are also either right-eyed or left-eyed? Your brain prefers one eye over the other.

Look at something far away and point your finger at it. Now close your left eye. Now close just your right eye. Your finger will appear to jump!

The eye that is open when your finger does not jump is your dominant eye. Use it when you're taking pictures.

Floating Pencil

Grab a pencil like this:

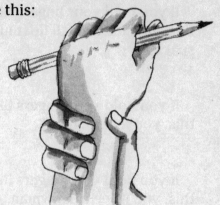

Make sure you are secretly holding the pencil with the index finger of your other hand.

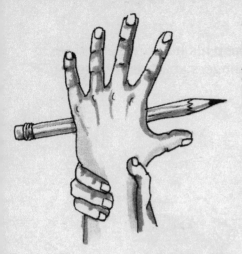

Slowly open your fingers. The pencil looks like it's floating!

Just don't let anyone see your tricky finger in the back.

Finger Power

Have a friend clasp his hands together, holding his index fingers apart as wide as possible.

With your finger, trace a circle around your friend's fingers. Keep tracing this circle very fast, over and over.

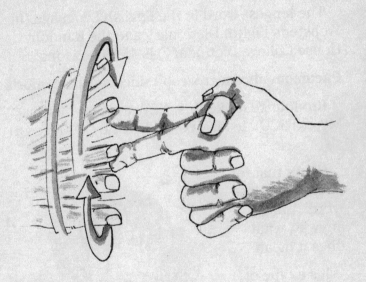

Mysteriously, your friend's fingers will slowly come together!

Actually, your friend's fingers would come together, anyway, because his finger muscles would eventually get tired. But don't tell him that!

The Longest Word

No, it's not "Supercalifragilisticexpialidocious." That's a Mary Poppins word, not a dictionary word.

The longest word in the English Language (in Webster's Eighth Dictionary and the Random House College Dictionary) is 45 letters long:

Pneumonoultramicroscopicsilicovolcanoconiosis

Pronounce it like this: NEW mon oh UL tra MY cro SCOP ic SIL i co vol KAY no CONE ee OH sis.

How's that for a totally useless word! And anyway, what does it mean?

It's a type of disease that you get when you pronounce long words.

No, really, it's a lung disease that coal miners get when they breathe ultramicroscopic particles of sand as they dig through volcanic rock.

Little Secret

STEP BY STEP

Sometimes a skill is too complicated or too large to learn all at once. It's easier if you first break the large skill into smaller skills, and then learn it step by step.

So, don't try to pronounce

"pneumonoultramicroscopicsilicovolcanoconiosis"

all at once. Learn it step by step:

1) pneumono (NEW mon oh)

2) ultra (UL tra)

3) microscopic (MY cro SCOP ic)

4) silico (SIL i co)

5) volcano (vol KAY no)

6) coniosis (CONE ee OH sis)

It's faster to master six small skills than one large skill!

Tingly Hands

Rub your hands together, very fast, until they are warm. Now keep rubbing them until they are hot. Keep it up, even faster!

When your hands are so hot you can hardly stand it, hold them exactly as if you were holding a basketball, like this:

You will feel an odd tingling between your hands! THIS IS A WEIRD FEELING!

Mismatched Fingers

Close your eyes and spread your arms straight out to the side.

Now try to touch your index fingers over your head.

Maybe you can get it on the second or third try, but probably not on the first.

Leap Through Paper

Did you know you can jump right through a sheet of paper?

Fold a piece of paper and make cuts as close to the edge of the paper as possible, like this. Don't cut all the way through.

Turn the paper over and cut *between* the original cuts, cutting as close to the fold as possible. Be sure to skip over the first and last end cuts.

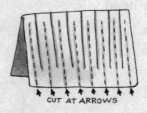

CUT AT ARROWS

Carefully unfold the paper. Cut along the crease between the first and last slits, as shown. Notice that you don't cut the paper at the top or the bottom.

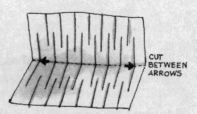

CUT BETWEEN ARROWS

Now slowly spread it open, and jump right through!

Using the same method, you can stick your head through a business card or march your school band through a newspaper.

Little Secret

MAKE IT INTERESTING

As you've just seen, you can make even the most ordinary objects interesting. The more interesting something is—like a skill—the easier it is to learn.

Do you like baseball, but hate math? Then chances are you'll have an easier time learning baseball than learning math.

But it's possible to learn mathematics better—by using baseball! You can improve your math skills by figuring batting averages, league standings, speeds of fastballs, and better batting orders.

Why? Because learning is easier if you make it interesting.

31

A Steel Grip

Challenge your dad or mom to pull your hand off your head. Neither will be able to do it.

Your parents can only use one hand, and they must lift straight up. They can't pull to the side, and no jerking allowed.

32

They can't do it because you are using your biceps muscle and they are using their triceps muscle. The biceps muscle is stronger than the triceps muscle.

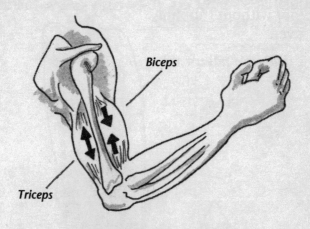

Little Secret
REST

How are you doing so far? Need a break? Good idea! Because scientists have discovered that you can learn a skill better by resting!

"WHAAAT!! You can learn better by not doing anything?"

That's right. Learning something is easier if you practice in short sessions with rests in between, rather than practicing in one long session.

Totally Useless Skills

We All Fall Down

Stand with your left shoulder and left foot right up against a wall. Now try lifting the right foot without toppling over.

Did you fall for it?

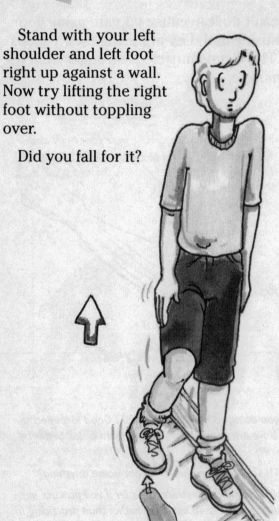

(By the way, this works just as well—or as badly—if you reverse things, so that you're using your right side and lifting your left foot.)

Did You Know?

Everyone has a center of gravity. It's inside your body and about three inches above your belly button. Half your weight is above this spot, and half is below. Also, half your weight is to the right, and half is to the left.

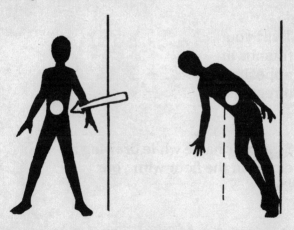

If your feet are not under your center of gravity (like when you stood against the wall and lifted your foot), you will fall down.

If you are doing two different things at the same time, then you are doing a "Boggler." The classic boggler is rubbing your stomach while patting your head.

If you've already mastered that, here are some other bogglers to try . . .

- Twirl your thumbs in opposite directions.

- Sign your name while drawing a circle on the floor with your foot.

- Brush your teeth and comb your hair at the same time.

- Nod your head and say "no." Shake your head and say "yes."

- Draw a triangle in the air with one hand. Draw a square in the air with the other. Now do both at the same time.

Little Secret

STOP, THINK, GO

Many skills are easier to master if you stop and think before you go.

So try the last skill again, only this time don't try to do it all at once.

First stop and think of just one line from the triangle, and one line from the square. Don't draw them. Just picture them in your mind.

Okay, now go and draw these two lines. Then stop. Now think of the next line on each shape.

Go and draw them, then stop. Now think of the next lines. Go, then stop. And so on.

Can't Meet Pencils

Stretch your arms out and hold two pencils in front of you. Point the tips at each other. Close one eye. Now try to touch the pencil tips together.

Did You Know?

We need both eyes to judge distances. So if you close one eye your brain cannot easily tell how far each pencil is from you.

The Invisible Ball

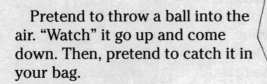

Hold a paper bag at the top edge between the thumb and second finger.

Pretend to throw a ball into the air. "Watch" it go up and come down. Then, pretend to catch it in your bag.

At the moment your invisible ball "enters" your bag, SNAP THE FINGERS THAT ARE HOLDING THE BAG. (Do this without letting go of the bag.)

The sound of the snap will sound like the ball has landed in the bag.

Chair Pick-Up

Stand against a wall and step backward, measuring off three foot lengths.

Pull a lightweight chair in front of you, or have someone slide it over. Bend at the waist so that your head is against the wall and over the chair.

Now try lifting the chair and standing up.

It's easy . . . if you're a girl. But guys can't do it! Guys just won't be able to stand up.

Why? Because girls generally have shorter feet than boys. When girls try this skill, their three steps backward do not take them as far from the wall as boys. So when they lean over, their feet are directly under their center of gravity.

When boys try this, *their* three steps backward take them farther from the wall than girls. When they lean over, their center of gravity is not directly over their feet. In fact, if the wall wasn't there, they'd fall down!

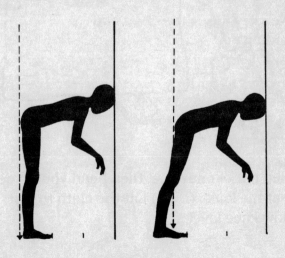

The Disappearing Leg

Cover yourself from the waist down with a large cloth. (Don't let more than the tips of your shoes show.)

Slip out of one shoe, then bend your shoeless leg at the knee. (Duh!) Lift the cloth to just below knee level.

Now, to bring it back . . .

Lower the cloth to the floor again.

Slip back into your shoe. Don't let anyone see your shoe move!

With your best bullfighter imperson- ation, fling the cloth aside to reveal your "restored" leg. (This is a good one to practice in front of a friend.)

Fake Spoon Bending

This is a great trick to try at important dinners like Thanksgiving, when the grown-ups like to haul out their best silverware.

To start, get a spoon and hold it so that your audience views it from the front.

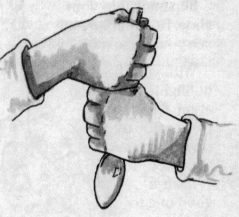

Be sure not to grip the spoon with your thumbs. Keep them out of the way of your fingers.

Push your top hand forward, and at the same time pull your bottom hand backward to let the spoon handle slowly pass downward through your fingers. (Try to keep your hands upright.)

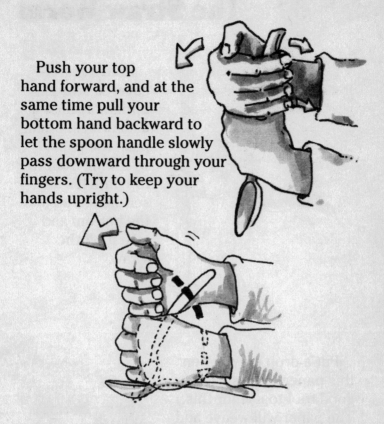

Make a face while you're doing this skill. That way your audience will think you're struggling a little, and the spoon bending will seem even more realistic.

The Straw Worm

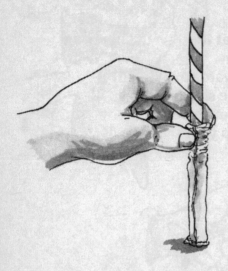

Hold a paper-covered straw upright against a flat surface. Then, push the paper wrapping from the top until it's all scrunched up at the bottom and take it off the straw.

Put a drop of water on this paper. (The straw is a good tool to use for this.) The paper will weave and wiggle like a worm.

Hole in Your Hand

With your left eye, look though a tube or any rolled-up paper. Hold your right hand against the tube and about 9 inches away from your nose. Keep both eyes open.

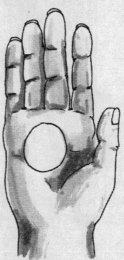

You'll see a hole in your hand!

Floating Arms

Stand in a doorway and press the backs of your hands against the frame.

Count to twenty. Keep pressing. When you reach twenty-one, relax.

When you walk away, you'll feel your arms floating up!

Stick 'Em Up!

Touch one, two, three, or four fingers to your friend's back. Ask him to guess how many fingers you're using.

Most of his guesses will be wrong.

Now ask your friend to close his eyes. This time, put one, two, three, or four fingers against the palm of his hand. Ask him to guess how many fingers you're touching to his palm.

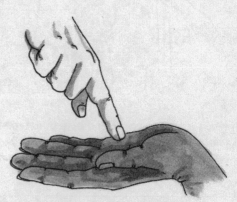

His guess will almost always be right!

Did You Know?

The nerve endings on the back are spread far apart, like this:

But the nerve endings on the hand are bunched up very closely, like this:

When you touch your friend's back, his brain receives less information than it does when you touch his hand. With less information his brain has a harder time figuring out how many fingers are touching.

Funny Money

Tell your parents you'll be good forever if they just give you $26.

After they say, "WHAAAAAT!," tell them, "Okay, okay, I won't be good forever, but would you *loan* me a twenty-dollar bill, a five-dollar bill, and a one-dollar bill for just a few minutes?"

After they give in, fold each bill in half, the long way.

Now you can hold the bills together in different ways to make funny presidential portraits.

Abraham Washington

George Jackson

Andrew Lincoln

Did You Know?

George Washington, Andrew Jackson, and Abraham Lincoln were three of our greatest presidents, but did you know they were also great failures at different times in their lives?

As a general, Washington lost more battles than he won. Jackson failed to win the first time he ran for president. And Lincoln was once a flop as a store owner.

What was their secret for becoming successful? They kept trying. Sound familiar?

The
BIG SECRET

You skipped to this part, right? If you did then I have to tell you some little secrets I talked about in the book. They are little learning secrets.

- *Try*

- *Keep trying*

- *Try new ways*

- *Make it interesting*

- *Read*

- *Two are better than one*

- *Stop . . . think . . . go*

- *Step by step*

- *Rest*

- *Go slowly*

Now the Real
BIG SECRET
is:

IF YOU USE THESE LITTLE SECRETS, YOU CAN LEARN ANYTHING YOU WANT TO DO.

- *Do you want to do incredible skateboard stunts? KEEP TRYING!*

- *Do you want to be a veterinarian? READ!*

- *Do you want to be better at video games? TRY NEW WAYS!*

- *Do you want to be a scientist? MAKE IT INTERESTING!*

- *Do you want to play piano? GO SLOWLY!*

I think you have the idea, you genius, you.

Join the Institute of Totally Useless Skills

The Institute of Totally Useless Skills is an organization devoted to bringing to humanity a bunch of skills that have absolutely no practical value, but that indirectly promote self-esteem, coordination, concentration, persistence, and FUN!

Now you can become the newest member in the famous Institute of Totally Useless Skills. Just send a self-addressed stamped envelope to us, and in return we'll send you a free membership card.

Do you know a totally useless skill? We'd like to know it, too! So, please send it in and share it with us. If we've never seen your skill before, we may ask you if we can put it in our next book. If we do, you'll get a free copy. Such a deal!

Write to:

The Institute of Totally Useless Skills
P.O. Box 181
Temple, NH 03084

WANTED!

HAVE YOU SEEN THIS PERSON'S MIND?

It's been missing since 1950. It used to belong to Rick Davis, the author of this book. He was last seen performing at DisneyWorld, on Broadway, at the Ringling Brothers Circus, at the White House, and at fine schools everywhere.

He has been described as a middle-aged kid trying to find his adult self. He is known to do things just for fun. He is also known as the president of the Institute of Totally Useless Skills.

(By the way, if you find this person's mind, please do not return it. The author reports that he's getting along fine without it.)

Diploma
THE INSTITUTE OF
TOTALLY USELESS SKILLS

hereby confers upon

_____

(fill in your name)

the Degree of P.U.

(Practitioner Of Uselessness)

for needlessly mastering the following talents:

Arm Stretching	Arm Shrinking	Disappear Your Teacher's Head
Split Pencil	Mystery In The Middle	Nose Breaking
Balancing Act	Ghost Pencil	Spoon Hanging
Hot Dog!	Floating Pencil	Finger Power
Magnetic Pencils	The Longest Word	Tingly Hands
Leap Through Paper	A Steel Grip	We All Fall Down
Bogglers	Mismatched Fingers	Can't Meet Pencils
Chair Pick-up	The Disappearing Leg	The Invisible Ball
Fake Spoon Bending	The Straw Worm	Floating Arms
Hole In Your Hand	Stick 'Em Up	Funny Money

THIS DIPLOMA ENTITLES YOU TO ABSOLUTELY NOTHING, BUT DOES PROVIDE SOMETHING HANDY TO WRAP YOUR BUBBLEGUM IN.

In witness thereof, this document has been pointlessly signed by a person with absolutely no authority whatsoever.

Rick Davis

Rick Davis
Master of Uselessness